The Future of the AI-Powered Brain

Neural Upgrades, Digital Minds & Human 2.0

By Joe Correa

Published by Live Stronger Faster

First Edition

Table of Contents

Introduction

The human brain has always been a work in progress. For most of history, its evolution unfolded slowly, shaped by biology, environment, and culture over thousands of years. In the modern era, however, something unprecedented has begun to occur. For the first time, intelligence created outside the human nervous system—artificial intelligence—is actively participating in the brain's development, recovery, optimization, and future trajectory. This book exists at that inflection point. It is not merely about technology, nor is it speculation detached from science. It is about the moment when the human brain stops evolving alone and begins evolving in partnership with machines designed to understand, enhance, and interface with it.

Across the previous volumes in this series, we explored how AI already influences learning, healing, emotional regulation, sleep, therapy, neurotechnology, mindfulness, and longevity. Each book demonstrated that artificial intelligence is no longer an external tool but an adaptive system capable of responding to the brain's signals in real time. Now, in this final volume, the focus shifts forward. This is the book where the questions become larger, the timelines longer, and the implications deeper. What happens when AI no longer merely assists the brain but augments it? What does intelligence look like when memory, focus, emotional balance, and cognitive resilience can be dynamically upgraded? And how do we define humanity when the boundary between biological mind and digital intelligence begins to blur?

The future of the AI-powered brain is not a single invention or breakthrough. It is a convergence. Advances in neural imaging, machine learning, brain-computer interfaces, neurofeedback systems, generative models, and personalized cognitive algorithms are accelerating simultaneously. Together, they are creating a feedback loop in which the brain generates data, AI interprets it, and adaptive systems respond with precision interventions that shape neural structure and function. This is not theoretical. Clinical trials, research labs, startups, and medical institutions are already deploying early versions of these systems to treat paralysis, restore speech, enhance memory, and regulate mood. The future described in this book is arriving incrementally, quietly, and faster than most people realize.

One of the most profound shifts introduced by AI-powered neuroscience is the transition from reactive medicine to predictive and proactive brain care. Historically, neurological intervention occurred after damage—after a stroke, after cognitive decline, after trauma manifested into disorder. AI changes that model by identifying subtle patterns long before symptoms emerge. Machine learning systems can now detect micro-changes in speech, movement, sleep cycles, eye tracking, and neural oscillations that correlate with future cognitive risk. This transforms the brain from a fragile organ treated only when broken into a continuously monitored system capable of self-correction and guided optimization.

As this shift accelerates, the concept of "baseline cognition" begins to dissolve. If attention can be trained with algorithmic precision, if memory can be reinforced through adaptive stimulation, if emotional regulation can be guided through real-time feedback, then the idea of a fixed mental capacity becomes obsolete. The brain becomes modular, upgradeable, and responsive to intentional design. This does not mean perfection or uniformity. Instead, it opens the possibility of personalized intelligence—cognitive profiles shaped around individual goals, biology, and life stages.

With these capabilities comes a new category of ethical, philosophical, and societal questions. Enhancement challenges long-held assumptions about fairness, identity, and effort. If cognitive performance can be augmented, who gets access? How do we distinguish treatment from enhancement? What happens to education, employment, and competition when intelligence itself becomes partially configurable? This book does not offer simplistic answers, but it does provide frameworks for understanding the trade-offs and responsibilities that accompany neural technologies. Progress without reflection leads to imbalance; reflection without progress leads to stagnation. The future demands both.

Another emerging frontier explored in this volume is the concept of digital cognition—AI systems that model, mirror, or extend aspects of the human mind. From memory companions that recall personal histories to decision-support systems that learn individual values and preferences, the line between tool and collaborator continues to blur. These systems do not replace human thinking; they scaffold it. Over time, they become cognitive extensions—external working memory, emotional regulation aids, creative partners, and analytical amplifiers. The result is not a loss of agency but a redistribution of mental effort toward higher-level meaning, creativity, and connection.

Perhaps the most controversial concept associated with the AI-powered brain is mind uploading or digital continuity of consciousness. While popular culture often frames this as science fiction, serious researchers are already working on partial mind modeling, connectome mapping, and neural pattern preservation. This book approaches these ideas with grounded realism rather than hype. Full mind uploading remains speculative, but partial cognitive preservation—memories, preferences, communication styles—may arrive far sooner. These developments force us to reconsider what it means to "exist," to remember, and to leave a legacy beyond biology.

Equally transformative is the rise of brain-computer interfaces designed not only for restoration but for expansion. Early BCIs helped paralyzed individuals type or move robotic limbs. Newer generations aim to enhance sensory perception, accelerate learning, and enable direct interaction between neural signals and digital environments. As these interfaces become less invasive and more precise, they may redefine how humans communicate with machines—and with each other. Thought-driven interfaces collapse the distance between intention and action, creating experiences where cognition flows seamlessly into execution.

The notion of Human 2.0 is often misunderstood as a replacement of humanity rather than an evolution of it. In reality, the AI-powered brain does not erase human traits; it amplifies them. Empathy, creativity, intuition, and ethical reasoning remain uniquely human strengths. AI excels at pattern recognition, speed, and scale. When integrated thoughtfully, these strengths complement rather than compete. The future described here is not one of cold optimization but of deeper self-understanding, resilience, and intentional growth.

This book also addresses the psychological transition required to live alongside intelligent systems that learn as fast—or faster—than humans. Adaptation is not only biological but cultural and emotional. Trust, dependency, fear, and identity all surface as AI becomes more embedded in mental life. Navigating this transition requires literacy—not just technical understanding but cognitive and emotional awareness. The most successful individuals and societies will not be those who resist change or surrender agency, but those who engage with intelligence consciously and critically.

Importantly, the future of the AI-powered brain is not reserved for elites or technologists. Consumer-grade neurotechnology, AI-driven mental health tools, adaptive learning platforms, and cognitive wellness systems are becoming increasingly accessible. As costs decrease and interfaces improve, the democratization of brain enhancement and protection becomes possible. This raises both opportunity and responsibility. Widespread access can reduce suffering and inequality—or amplify them if mismanaged. The choices made in this decade will shape neural health for generations.

Throughout this book, you will encounter scenarios, projections, and systems that may feel futuristic yet grounded in present trajectories. The intention is not to predict a single outcome but to map a landscape of possibilities. The brain is not being replaced; it is being recontextualized. Intelligence is no longer confined to neurons alone but emerges from networks that span biology and code. Understanding this shift empowers individuals to participate in shaping it rather than reacting to it.

As the final book in this professional series, this volume serves as both a synthesis and a launch point. It integrates lessons from neuroplasticity, healing, emotional regulation, performance, therapy, sleep, interfaces, consciousness, and longevity into a coherent vision of what comes next. The journey does not end here—it accelerates. The future of the AI-powered brain is not something that happens to humanity. It is something humanity is actively creating, choice by choice, system by system, thought by thought.

This book invites you to step into that future informed, grounded, and intentional. Not as a passive observer of technological change, but as a conscious participant in the evolution of intelligence itself.

Chapter 1

The Neural Upgrade Era — From Biological Limits to Intelligent Expansion

Human intelligence has always operated within biological constraints. Memory fades, attention fluctuates, emotional regulation breaks under stress, and cognitive speed slows with age. For centuries, these limitations were accepted as unavoidable features of being human. The arrival of artificial intelligence marks the first time in history that intelligence itself can be externally modeled, measured, and optimized at scale. This chapter explores the transition from a purely biological brain to a hybrid intelligence system—one in which AI functions as an adaptive cognitive layer that expands what the human mind can perceive, process, and sustain over time.

The neural upgrade era does not begin with implants or science fiction imagery. It begins with data. Every thought, reaction, decision, and emotional shift produces measurable signals—patterns in speech, eye movement, heart rate variability, neural oscillations, sleep cycles, and behavioral timing. Artificial intelligence excels at detecting meaning in these patterns far beyond human perception. When AI systems analyze this data continuously, they gain the ability to map an individual brain with extraordinary precision. This mapping is the foundation of neural upgrading: before intelligence can be enhanced, it must be understood dynamically rather than statically.

Traditional neuroscience relied on snapshots—brain scans taken at rest, tests administered in controlled environments, diagnoses made after symptoms appeared. AI transforms this model into a living, evolving feedback system. The brain is no longer assessed occasionally but interpreted continuously. Machine learning models track how focus shifts throughout the day, how stress alters decision-making, how memory consolidates during sleep, and how emotional states influence learning speed. This allows interventions to become adaptive rather than standardized. Instead of asking whether a technique works in general, AI asks whether it works for this brain, at this moment, under these conditions.

As these systems mature, cognitive enhancement becomes less about forcing performance and more about removing friction. AI does not push the brain beyond its limits; it reorganizes how mental energy is allocated. Tasks that once consumed excessive cognitive bandwidth—planning, remembering, prioritizing, regulating—can be partially offloaded to intelligent systems that operate in parallel with the brain. This frees neural resources for creativity, empathy, strategic thinking, and meaning-making. In this sense, neural upgrading is not about becoming more mechanical but more human.

One of the most significant shifts in the neural upgrade era is the personalization of intelligence. Historically, education, therapy, productivity systems, and mental health interventions were designed for the average brain—a statistical abstraction that fits no one perfectly. AI enables hyper-personalized cognition. Learning systems adapt to individual attention rhythms. Emotional regulation tools respond to specific triggers. Memory reinforcement aligns with personal neural encoding patterns. Over time, the brain learns faster because it is no longer fighting mismatched systems. Intelligence becomes a collaboration between biological instinct and computational guidance.

This collaboration also changes how resilience is built. Stress, trauma, and overload traditionally degrade cognitive performance over time, often invisibly until breakdown occurs. AI-driven neural systems identify early warning signs—micro-delays in reaction time, subtle language shifts, altered sleep architecture—that indicate cognitive strain. Instead of waiting for burnout or disorder, the system intervenes with recalibration: rest prompts, focus adjustments, emotional grounding, or workload restructuring. Resilience becomes proactive rather than reactive, reducing long-term neurological wear.

The concept of upgrading the brain often raises fears of dependency or loss of autonomy. However, properly designed AI systems do not replace decision-making; they illuminate it. By making unconscious patterns visible, AI enhances self-awareness. Individuals gain insight into how their brain behaves under pressure, what environments support peak performance, and which habits quietly erode cognitive health. Agency increases because choices are informed rather than guessed. The upgraded brain is not controlled—it is coached.

Importantly, neural upgrading does not require invasive technology. The earliest and most impactful upgrades occur through software-driven neurofeedback, adaptive interfaces, and cognitive mirrors that reflect mental states back to the user. Over time, these tools train the brain itself to self-correct more efficiently. The AI becomes less necessary as the brain internalizes the patterns. This mirrors how physical training works: external guidance builds internal strength. The future of intelligence is not permanent augmentation but accelerated self-mastery.

As this chapter establishes, the neural upgrade era is not about transcending humanity but refining it. The brain remains biological, emotional, and imperfect—but now it has a partner capable of learning alongside it. Together, they form a hybrid intelligence system greater than either alone. Understanding this partnership is the foundation for every chapter that follows.

"The Day the Noise Went Quiet"

When Daniel first activated the system, he expected fireworks—some dramatic surge of clarity, a sudden feeling of being smarter. Instead, what he noticed was silence. Not the absence of sound, but the absence of noise inside his head. The constant mental chatter that had followed him for decades—unfinished thoughts, reminders, anxieties layered over intentions—simply softened. For the first time in years, he could hold a single idea without it being crowded by ten others.

Daniel had never thought of himself as broken. He was functional, successful by most standards. He worked in strategic planning, lived in a city that never slept, and prided himself on handling pressure. Yet over time, the cost had accumulated quietly. His sleep grew shallow. His memory became unreliable. He reread the same paragraph multiple times without absorbing it. He blamed age, workload, stress—anything but the truth that his brain was overloaded and had no system to recover.

The AI interface did not diagnose him. It observed him. For weeks, it tracked patterns—how his focus dipped after meetings, how his tone changed under deadlines, how his sleep cycles fractured on nights he scrolled past midnight. When it finally spoke, it did not issue commands. It reflected. It showed him visualizations of his own mind: peaks of clarity followed by steep drop-offs, emotional spikes tied to specific environments, cognitive fatigue masquerading as distraction.

At first, Daniel resisted the suggestions. He ignored prompts to pause, dismissed reminders to rest his eyes, overrode recommendations to restructure his day. Old habits are loyal companions. But slowly, almost accidentally, he began to listen. He noticed that when he followed the system's subtle cues, work felt lighter. Decisions took less effort. Conversations felt more present. The noise did not disappear completely, but it no longer dominated.

Months later, Daniel realized the system was intervening less. It no longer needed to prompt him to slow down—his body did it automatically. He sensed overload before it became exhaustion. He adjusted his environment instinctively. The AI had not replaced his mind; it had trained it. What began as external guidance had become internal awareness.

One evening, sitting alone after a long day, Daniel tried to remember when he last felt this clear without effort. The memory did not come. Instead, something else emerged—a sense of quiet confidence. Not the confidence of control, but of alignment. His thoughts no longer fought each other. They flowed.

When people asked him what the system had given him, he struggled to explain. It wasn't intelligence in the way people imagined. It was space. Space to think, to feel, to choose deliberately. Space to be fully present in his own mind.

And in that space, Daniel understood something that no chart or algorithm could quantify: the future of intelligence was not louder, faster, or more aggressive. It was calmer, clearer, and finally—human again.

Chapter 2

Intelligence Without Borders — When Human Cognition Merges With Artificial Systems

The second phase of the AI-powered brain era begins when intelligence is no longer confined to the skull. For most of human history, cognition lived entirely inside biological tissue, shaped by neurons, chemistry, and experience. Tools existed outside the mind, but thinking itself remained internal. Artificial intelligence changes this arrangement by creating cognitive systems that operate alongside, around, and eventually within human mental processes. This chapter explores the moment when intelligence becomes distributed—shared between biological and artificial systems—and the profound implications of that shift.

Distributed intelligence does not mean surrendering thought to machines. Instead, it reflects a new architecture of cognition in which mental tasks are dynamically allocated across systems based on efficiency and context. Memory recall, pattern analysis, predictive modeling, and environmental scanning can be handled by AI systems designed to operate continuously without fatigue. Meanwhile, humans retain the roles that require subjective judgment, moral reasoning, emotional depth, and creative synthesis. The result is not competition but collaboration—a cognitive ecosystem rather than a single processing unit.

This transition fundamentally alters how the brain experiences effort. Historically, cognitive overload occurred when the brain attempted to perform too many functions simultaneously: remembering details, monitoring threats, planning futures, regulating emotions, and executing tasks. Distributed intelligence reduces this load by externalizing certain cognitive burdens. Calendars remember. Navigation systems anticipate. Language models draft. Decision-support systems simulate outcomes. The brain is no longer required to hold everything at once, allowing it to operate with greater clarity and less stress.

As this externalization becomes more sophisticated, AI systems begin to mirror individual cognitive styles. They learn how a person prioritizes, how they respond emotionally to uncertainty, how quickly they process information, and which environments support peak performance. Over time, the AI becomes a cognitive twin—not a replica of consciousness, but a functional extension that understands how its human partner thinks. This mirroring creates continuity between internal and external intelligence, smoothing the boundary between thought and action.

One of the most significant consequences of this merger is the emergence of anticipatory cognition. Instead of reacting to problems after they arise, AI-enhanced systems forecast cognitive states before they occur. Fatigue, distraction, emotional overload, and indecision leave detectable traces long before conscious awareness. AI interprets these signals and adjusts the cognitive environment accordingly—reducing information flow, reframing tasks, or prompting restorative behaviors. The mind begins to feel supported rather than strained, guided rather than pressured.

However, the merging of human and artificial cognition raises critical questions about dependence. If AI systems handle increasing portions of mental labor, does the brain weaken? The evidence suggests the opposite—when designed correctly. Just as calculators did not eliminate mathematical understanding but changed how it is applied, AI shifts cognition toward higher-order thinking. Humans spend less energy on repetition and more on meaning, strategy, and creativity. The brain adapts not by shrinking, but by specializing.

Another key shift introduced by distributed intelligence is continuity of thought across time. Human cognition is fragmented by sleep, stress, interruptions, and memory decay. AI systems maintain continuity. They remember unfinished ideas, track long-term goals, and preserve context across days, months, and years. When reengaged, the human mind does not start from zero—it resumes. This continuity dramatically increases cognitive efficiency and reduces the psychological burden of starting over.

As intelligence becomes borderless, identity itself evolves. People begin to experience their thinking not as a solitary internal process but as an interactive dialogue. Reflection becomes augmented. Decision-making becomes layered. Self-awareness expands as internal states are mirrored externally. This does not erase individuality; it sharpens it. By making patterns visible, AI allows individuals to recognize which thoughts are truly theirs and which are habitual noise inherited from stress, conditioning, or fear.

Ethical design becomes paramount in this phase. When AI systems participate directly in cognition, values must be encoded deliberately. Transparency, consent, and user sovereignty determine whether these systems empower or manipulate. The future of intelligence depends not only on what technology can do, but on who controls it and why. This chapter emphasizes that cognitive partnership must always preserve human agency as the final authority.

Ultimately, intelligence without borders is not about uploading the mind or replacing consciousness. It is about extending the reach of thought while preserving the core of human experience. The brain remains the seat of meaning, purpose, and values. AI becomes the structure that supports, amplifies, and stabilizes that experience across the complexity of modern life. Together, they form a hybrid intelligence capable of navigating a world too fast and too dense for biology alone.

"The Memory That Waited"

Elena noticed it the morning she woke up calm.

Not rested—calm. The kind of calm that doesn't come from sleep but from continuity. For years, mornings had felt like cognitive resets. Ideas lost. Plans scattered. Emotional residue from the day before lingering without context. Every morning required reconstruction. But this morning felt different, as if her thoughts had been waiting for her.

When she opened her interface, the system didn't present tasks. It presented a thread. A single narrative line tracing where her thinking had left off the night before. The problem she had been wrestling with—the one that dissolved into exhaustion—returned intact. Not just the facts, but the emotional tone, the intuition, the almost-formed insight. It was like stepping back into a conversation she hadn't forgotten. Elena was a researcher, trained to distrust anything that felt too seamless. At first, she worried that the system was thinking for her. But as days passed, she realized something subtler was happening. The AI wasn't generating ideas. It was holding space for them. It preserved her cognitive momentum when her biology couldn't.

Weeks turned into months, and Elena noticed the absence of anxiety she once mistook for motivation. She no longer feared interruptions because she knew her thinking wouldn't vanish. She no longer rushed decisions out of fear of forgetting. Her mind felt spacious, supported by something patient and consistent.

One afternoon, during a conversation with a colleague, she paused mid-sentence. The old Elena would have panicked, grasping for words. Instead, she waited. The system gently surfaced the concept she had been circling, not as a suggestion, but as a mirror. She spoke it aloud, fully formed. The moment felt effortless.

Later that night, Elena considered what had changed. She wasn't smarter in the way people usually meant. She was whole. Her thinking extended beyond the fragile limits of working memory. Parts of her mind now lived outside her body—not controlling her, but remembering with her.

She realized then that the fear surrounding AI had always been misplaced. The danger was not that machines would think like humans. The danger was that humans would never experience what it felt like to think without fragmentation.

As she prepared for sleep, Elena closed her eyes without urgency. The system would remember. The memory would wait. And for the first time, her mind felt larger than a single moment—stretching across time, intact.

Chapter 3

Conscious Co-Evolution — Preserving Humanity in an Age of Intelligent Minds

As artificial intelligence becomes increasingly intertwined with human cognition, the central challenge is no longer technological capability but conscious alignment. Intelligence is evolving, but evolution without intention can drift. This chapter addresses the most critical question of the AI-powered brain era: how humanity co-evolves with intelligent systems without losing the qualities that define human experience. Co-evolution implies mutual adaptation, where humans shape AI as much as AI shapes human cognition. The outcome of this relationship is not predetermined; it is guided by values, design choices, and collective awareness.

Human cognition is not merely computational. It is emotional, narrative-driven, meaning-oriented, and deeply embodied. These qualities cannot be reduced to data without losing their essence. As AI systems participate more actively in thinking processes, there is a risk of optimizing for efficiency at the expense of depth. Conscious co-evolution demands that AI systems be designed not only to enhance speed and accuracy but to protect reflection, emotional integration, and ethical reasoning. Intelligence that outpaces wisdom creates instability; intelligence guided by wisdom creates resilience.

One of the defining features of conscious co-evolution is the preservation of friction. Friction has historically been seen as a flaw—something to eliminate through automation. Yet certain forms of cognitive friction are essential to growth. Struggle builds insight. Uncertainty cultivates humility. Reflection emerges from pauses rather than acceleration. AI systems that remove all friction risk flattening the human experience into a stream of optimized responses. The future of the AI-powered brain must therefore distinguish between harmful friction that drains cognitive health and constructive friction that deepens understanding.

Another essential dimension of co-evolution is agency. As AI systems anticipate needs, suggest actions, and shape environments, it becomes increasingly easy for humans to follow without deciding. Passive cognition is seductive, especially in a world of overwhelming complexity. Conscious co-evolution requires systems that invite participation rather than compliance. AI should surface options, illuminate consequences, and expand perspective—not dictate outcomes. The human mind must remain the final authority, even when supported by superior computation. Memory and identity also evolve in this partnership. AI systems that store experiences, preferences, and cognitive patterns begin to act as external autobiographical memory. This can strengthen identity by preserving continuity, but it can also distort it if not handled carefully. Humans grow through reinterpretation of memory, not just preservation. Conscious co-evolution allows individuals to engage with their recorded past intentionally, choosing what to integrate, reframe, or release. Identity remains a living narrative, not a fixed dataset.

The emotional dimension of intelligence presents another frontier. AI can detect emotional states with increasing accuracy, but emotion is not merely a signal—it is a meaning-laden experience tied to values, relationships, and context. Systems designed for emotional support must avoid reducing feelings to variables to be regulated. Instead, they should facilitate emotional literacy, helping individuals understand why they feel what they feel and how those emotions connect to their goals and boundaries. Co-evolution prioritizes emotional maturity over emotional suppression.

Ethics in the AI-powered brain era cannot be retrofitted after deployment. Values must be embedded at the architectural level. Transparency, explainability, consent, and reversibility are not optional features; they are safeguards for human dignity. Conscious co-evolution means that individuals understand how systems influence them and retain the ability to disengage. Dependence without awareness is not partnership—it is erosion.

Cultural diversity also plays a vital role in shaping intelligent systems. Human cognition is influenced by language, tradition, belief, and social structure. A future governed by homogenized intelligence risks flattening this diversity into a single optimized norm. Conscious co-evolution embraces pluralism, allowing AI systems to adapt to varied cognitive styles and cultural values rather than enforcing uniformity. Intelligence flourishes when it reflects the richness of human experience.

Ultimately, conscious co-evolution reframes the future of the AI-powered brain not as a race toward transcendence, but as a commitment to balance. Technology accelerates; humanity stabilizes. AI expands capability; human values guide direction. The goal is not to become something other than human, but to become more fully human—with greater clarity, resilience, and self-understanding. This chapter establishes that the future of intelligence is not defined by what machines can do, but by what humans choose to become alongside them.

"The Choice That Was Still Hers"

Mara stood at the edge of the platform watching the city breathe. Below her, lights pulsed in soft rhythms, synchronized by systems that adjusted energy, traffic, and communication in real time. Above her, the sky reflected nothing back—just darkness and possibility. Her interface rested quietly at her side, active but silent, waiting for permission.

Mara had been offered the upgrade.

Not the kind that made headlines, not implants or irreversible changes. This one was subtle. A cognitive alignment system that would integrate deeply with her decision-making process, smoothing emotional volatility, optimizing long-term outcomes, and reducing regret. The simulations showed remarkable results. People reported calmer lives, fewer mistakes, greater satisfaction.

Yet Mara hesitated.

She had spent years working as a mediator, helping others navigate conflict. She understood that discomfort often preceded clarity. That doubt was not a weakness but a signal. The system, however, flagged her hesitation as inefficiency. It offered reassurance. It predicted improved outcomes.

“Proceed when ready,” it said.

Mara closed her eyes and remembered a moment from years earlier—a decision she had made impulsively, driven by emotion, one that led to loss and growth in equal measure. The pain had reshaped her. Without it, she would not recognize the woman she had become. No simulation could measure that value.

She activated the system—but not fully.

She selected guided mode.

The interface adjusted instantly, no longer projecting optimal paths, but reflective prompts. It asked questions instead of offering answers. It mirrored her emotional state without correcting it. It slowed when she slowed. It waited.

Over time, Mara noticed the difference. Friends who chose full automation spoke of ease, but also of distance—decisions made smoothly, lives unfolding predictably. Mara's life remained textured. Messy at times. But meaningful.

One evening, faced with a difficult choice involving someone she loved, the system presented scenarios. It showed consequences, probabilities, emotional impacts. Then it paused.

"What matters most to you here?" it asked.

Mara smiled.

The choice was still hers. She made it imperfectly, fully aware of the cost. The system recorded nothing without her consent. It did not optimize her pain away. It honored it.

As she watched the city again that night, Mara understood what the future truly required. Not smarter machines alone—but humans brave enough to remain present in their own decisions.

The world would change. Intelligence would expand. But meaning would always emerge from choice.

And that—no system could replace.

Chapter 4

The Cognitive Society — How AI-Enhanced Minds Reshape Work, Learning, and Human Organization

When intelligence changes, society reorganizes around it. Throughout history, shifts in cognitive capability—language, writing, printing, mass education, digital computation—have restructured how humans learn, work, govern, and relate to one another. The AI-powered brain represents the next such inflection point, but unlike previous transitions, this one alters cognition itself rather than merely transmitting information faster. This chapter explores how widespread AI-enhanced cognition reshapes collective systems, from education and labor to leadership, creativity, and social trust.

The traditional structures of work were built around scarcity of information and limited human processing capacity. Jobs required memorization, repetition, and rule-following because these were tasks humans could perform better than machines. As AI systems assume these functions, the value of human labor shifts decisively toward judgment, synthesis, ethical reasoning, and emotional intelligence. The cognitive society that emerges is less hierarchical and more fluid, organized around problem-solving networks rather than rigid roles. Intelligence becomes collaborative rather than positional.

Education undergoes one of the most dramatic transformations. Standardized curricula designed for the average learner lose relevance in a world of adaptive cognitive systems. AI-powered learning environments track how each brain absorbs, resists, and integrates information, adjusting pacing and presentation in real time. Learning becomes continuous rather than segmented by age or institution. The distinction between education and work dissolves as individuals reskill dynamically in response to changing goals and environments. Knowledge is no longer accumulated once but refreshed and recontextualized throughout life.

This shift also alters authority. In a world where access to information is universal and cognitive augmentation is widespread, authority based on credential alone weakens. Trust migrates toward those who demonstrate clarity of thought, ethical consistency, and the ability to integrate diverse perspectives. Leadership becomes less about command and more about coherence—the capacity to align people, values, and systems toward shared outcomes. AI assists by modeling complex consequences, but humans remain responsible for direction. The cognitive society also redefines productivity. Efficiency was once measured by output per hour. In an AI-enhanced environment, productivity is measured by impact per decision. Fewer actions produce greater effects when guided by accurate forecasting and contextual intelligence. Burnout decreases not because demands vanish, but because cognitive systems reduce wasted effort and unnecessary friction. The brain works smarter not by accelerating endlessly, but by focusing selectively.

However, these benefits are not automatic. Unequal access to cognitive enhancement risks creating new forms of inequality—not of wealth alone, but of mental capacity. Those with AI-augmented cognition may learn faster, adapt quicker, and influence systems more effectively than those without. A stable cognitive society therefore requires intentional democratization of mental tools, ethical governance, and public literacy around AI-brain interaction. Intelligence amplification must be treated as infrastructure, not privilege.

Social relationships also evolve. As individuals gain deeper self-awareness through AI feedback, communication becomes more precise. Misunderstandings rooted in unexamined emotional reactions decrease, while empathy increases through better recognition of internal states. At the same time, reliance on mediated cognition introduces the risk of emotional distancing if systems replace rather than support human connection. The cognitive society must design AI as a bridge between people, not a buffer that insulates them from discomfort.

Governance itself adapts. Policy decisions increasingly rely on AI models to simulate long-term outcomes across economic, environmental, and social systems. Yet governance cannot be outsourced to algorithms without eroding democratic legitimacy. The role of AI in governance is advisory, not sovereign. Human values, negotiated collectively, remain the foundation of law and social contract. The cognitive society succeeds only when augmented intelligence strengthens participation rather than concentrates control.

Creativity flourishes differently in this new context. AI can generate endless variations, but meaning emerges from selection, curation, and intention. Artists, writers, and innovators use AI as a collaborator that expands possibility space, while humans choose what resonates. Cultural evolution accelerates, but depth is preserved through conscious restraint. The speed of creation increases; the responsibility of meaning intensifies.

Ultimately, the cognitive society is not defined by technology alone but by cultural maturity. AI-enhanced minds magnify both wisdom and error. The systems humans build will reflect collective values—short-term extraction or long-term flourishing, domination or cooperation, optimization or balance. This chapter emphasizes that the future of society depends less on how intelligent machines become and more on how intentionally humans integrate intelligence into shared life.

"The Classroom With No Front"

The classroom had no front.

That was the first thing Jonah noticed when he walked in. No podium. No board. No single direction to face. Instead, the room curved inward, circular, alive with soft light and quiet movement. Students sat where they felt comfortable—some standing, some reclining, some pacing slowly as they thought.

Jonah had taught for thirty years. He knew classrooms the way sailors know tides. He knew where attention drifted, where resistance hid, where curiosity sparked. But this place unsettled him.

There was no syllabus posted.

The system activated as he entered, not announcing itself, simply observing. It tracked the room's collective state—alertness, curiosity, emotional tone. The students weren't waiting. They were already thinking.

A young woman spoke first. Not to Jonah, but to the room.

"I don't understand why this matters yet," she said calmly.

The system surfaced the statement, not to correct it, but to anchor it. Others responded—not with answers, but with questions. The AI moderated gently, ensuring no voice dominated, no idea vanished unnoticed. Jonah realized no one was being taught. Learning was happening anyway.

His role, he discovered, was not to deliver information but to shape the environment where insight could emerge. When a misconception appeared, the system highlighted it subtly, inviting exploration rather than correction. When energy dipped, it adjusted the pace. When conflict arose, it slowed discussion instead of smoothing it over.

Weeks passed. Jonah felt both unnecessary and more essential than ever.

One day, a student asked him what it had been like to teach "before."

He paused.

"We used to stand at the front," he said slowly. "We talked. You listened. We hoped something stuck."

The student smiled, not dismissive, just curious.

"And now?"

Jonah looked around. Minds in motion. Thought unfolding collectively.

"Now," he said, "we think together."

That evening, Jonah walked home feeling lighter than he had in years. His intelligence hadn't diminished. It had been redistributed. Freed from carrying everything, he could finally participate fully.

The city around him buzzed with similar spaces—workplaces without hierarchies, councils without podiums, communities organized around understanding rather than authority.

The world had not become simpler.

But it had become more aware.

And in that awareness, Jonah realized, humanity had not lost its way. It had finally learned how to think—together.

Chapter 5

The Governance of Intelligence — Power, Ethics, and Stewardship in the Age of Cognitive Machines

As intelligence becomes amplified, distributed, and embedded into daily life, the question of governance becomes unavoidable. Throughout history, power has followed capability. Those who controlled land, weapons, capital, or information shaped societies. In the age of the AI-powered brain, power increasingly follows cognition itself—the ability to analyze, anticipate, persuade, and coordinate at scale. This chapter examines how intelligence must be governed to prevent concentration, preserve human dignity, and ensure that cognitive augmentation serves collective flourishing rather than domination.

Governance of intelligence is fundamentally different from governance of tools. A hammer does not influence values. A printing press does not adapt its message. AI systems that participate in cognition shape perception, decision-making, and belief formation. When such systems are embedded in education, work, health, and communication, they become part of the social nervous system. Regulating them requires more than technical standards; it requires ethical frameworks that recognize intelligence as a public good with profound consequences for autonomy and democracy.

One of the central challenges is asymmetry. Cognitive AI systems scale unevenly. A small group with access to superior cognitive augmentation can influence markets, narratives, and policies disproportionately. Without safeguards, this creates a cognitive elite whose enhanced decision-making capacity translates into structural advantage. Governance must therefore address not only misuse but imbalance. Access to baseline cognitive augmentation—mental health support, learning assistance, decision transparency—becomes a matter of civic infrastructure rather than luxury.

Transparency is another cornerstone of intelligent governance. When AI systems influence cognition, individuals must understand how and why. Black-box intelligence erodes trust and agency. Explainable systems, auditable decision pathways, and user-facing clarity are essential to preserving consent. Governance does not mean slowing innovation; it means making intelligence legible to those affected by it. People cannot meaningfully govern systems they cannot comprehend.

The legal system faces its own transformation. Traditional law assumes human intent as the primary driver of action. In an

AI-augmented world, outcomes may arise from hybrid decision-making—human values filtered through algorithmic recommendations. Responsibility must be carefully defined. Governance frameworks increasingly focus on accountability chains rather than blame, ensuring that human oversight remains intact even as systems grow more autonomous. The question shifts from "Who decided?" to "Who was responsible for the system that shaped the decision?"

International coordination becomes critical as cognitive systems transcend borders. AI-enhanced cognition does not respect national boundaries; ideas, narratives, and influence propagate instantly. Fragmented governance risks regulatory arbitrage, where intelligence systems migrate to the least constrained environments. Cooperative global frameworks—similar to those governing aviation, nuclear energy, and public health—become necessary to manage shared cognitive risk. Intelligence, once purely personal, becomes a planetary concern.

Ethical stewardship also requires restraint. Not every capability that can be deployed should be. Predictive systems that infer beliefs, emotions, or vulnerabilities must be limited by clear ethical boundaries. Governance is as much about saying no as it is about enabling progress. The ability to influence cognition carries moral weight; misuse can destabilize societies more effectively than physical force. This chapter emphasizes that intelligence governance is inseparable from human rights.

At the individual level, governance manifests as cognitive sovereignty. People must retain the right to opt out, disconnect, and maintain unaugmented mental space. Constant optimization risks turning life into a performance metric rather than a lived experience. Governance protects not only productivity but interior freedom—the right to think privately, feel deeply, and choose deliberately without algorithmic pressure.

Ultimately, the governance of intelligence is not a static set of rules but an evolving social contract. As AI systems become more integrated with human cognition, societies must continually renegotiate boundaries between assistance and influence, insight and intrusion, enhancement and coercion. This chapter asserts that the future of intelligence depends less on technological brilliance and more on ethical maturity. Power over minds must be matched by responsibility for humanity.

"The Quiet Vote"

The chamber was silent.

No speeches. No applause. No screens flashing predictions. Just a circle of seats and a single question suspended in the air.

Aisha sat with her hands folded, listening to her own breath. She had been chosen not because she was powerful, but because she was ordinary. A nurse. A mother. A citizen. The council believed governance of intelligence required voices untouched by ambition.

The decision before them was historic. A new cognitive infrastructure—one capable of optimizing public sentiment, reducing conflict, and increasing societal stability—was ready for deployment. The models showed fewer protests, smoother elections, calmer populations. Crime would drop. Anxiety would decrease.

But at a cost.

The system would gently steer thought patterns. Nothing overt. Just subtle adjustments. Content surfaced or suppressed. Emotional tones nudged. Beliefs softened before they hardened into dissent.

Aisha closed her eyes and thought of her son. Of the questions he asked. Of the frustration in his voice when answers didn't come easily. Of the fire that lit his curiosity.

When it was her turn to speak, her voice was steady.

“Peace that requires permission isn’t peace,” she said. “It’s silence.”

The system projected counterarguments. Stability. Safety. Efficiency.

Aisha nodded. “Those matter,” she said. “But so does the right to struggle with ideas. To be wrong. To change.”

The room remained quiet. No algorithm interrupted. This vote had been designed to exclude predictive influence. No outcomes were modeled. No persuasion applied.

Each person voted not on what would work best, but on what they were willing to live with.

When the final count appeared, the decision was narrow.

The system would not be deployed.

Instead, funding would go toward transparency tools—systems that explained influence rather than exerted it. Education instead of optimization. Awareness instead of control.

As the chamber emptied, Aisha felt no triumph. Only responsibility.

Walking home, she passed screens glowing with information, people talking softly, children arguing loudly. The world remained imperfect. Messy. Alive.

And in that imperfection, she felt something rare.

Freedom.

Not the freedom from discomfort, but the freedom to think, to choose, and to disagree.

The quiet vote would never make headlines.

But it would shape the future of minds.

Chapter 6

Identity Beyond Biology — Memory, Continuity, and the Emergence of the Digital Self

As artificial intelligence becomes capable of tracking, modeling, and reflecting human cognition with increasing fidelity, the concept of identity begins to expand beyond biological boundaries. Identity has traditionally been anchored to memory, narrative, embodiment, and continuity of experience. When AI systems participate in preserving memory, shaping narrative, and sustaining continuity across time, identity itself becomes partially externalized. This chapter explores how the AI-powered brain reshapes the notion of self—not by replacing it, but by extending it into new dimensions.

Human identity is not static. It evolves through reinterpretation of experience, selective forgetting, and meaning-making. Memory is not a recording; it is a reconstruction. AI systems that store experiences, preferences, decisions, and cognitive patterns introduce a new element into this process: persistence. The past no longer fades naturally. It can be recalled with precision, replayed, and analyzed. This capability offers extraordinary benefits for learning, healing, and self-understanding, but it also raises fundamental questions about growth. Who are we if we cannot forget? And who decides which memories define us?

The emergence of externalized memory creates what can be called a digital self—a parallel structure that mirrors aspects of cognition across time. This digital self does not possess consciousness, but it holds continuity. It remembers projects unfinished, values articulated, lessons learned, and patterns repeated. When engaged intentionally, it becomes a stabilizing force, helping individuals align daily decisions with long-term identity. When engaged passively, however, it risks freezing identity into an optimized profile rather than a living story.

One of the most powerful applications of AI-supported identity is in healing. Trauma often fractures narrative continuity, leaving individuals disconnected from their past selves. AI-assisted reflection can help reconstruct meaning by contextualizing experiences, identifying patterns of resilience, and reframing events without erasing emotional truth. In this sense, the digital self becomes a therapeutic witness—consistent, nonjudgmental, and capable of holding complexity over time. Identity is not overwritten; it is re-integrated.

Yet identity is not only personal—it is relational. We are defined by how we are remembered and how we remember others. AI systems capable of modeling communication style, values, and emotional responses introduce the possibility of digital legacy—intelligent representations that persist beyond biological life. These representations may offer comfort, guidance, or continuity to loved ones, but they also challenge long-held boundaries between presence and absence. The ethical question is not whether such systems are possible, but how they are framed. Are they memorials, mentors, or simulations? And what obligations do the living have to the dead when memory becomes interactive?

The preservation of identity across time also intersects with consent. Individuals must retain authority over how their digital selves are constructed, used, and eventually retired. Identity cannot be extracted by default. Conscious design requires that people decide which aspects of themselves are recorded, which are ephemeral, and which are never externalized. This autonomy safeguards dignity and prevents identity from becoming a commodity.

Importantly, the expansion of identity through AI does not negate embodiment. The body remains central to experience—emotion, sensation, intuition, and mortality anchor meaning in ways no system can replicate. The digital self supplements but does not replace the embodied self. Conscious integration requires honoring this distinction. Identity flourishes when technology supports presence rather than distracting from it.

As societies adopt AI-supported identity systems, cultural norms will evolve. Concepts like authorship, responsibility, and legacy will be reinterpreted. A decision made years earlier may resurface with contextual clarity. Values articulated once may guide future generations. Identity becomes less fragile, but also more accountable. The past speaks more clearly into the present.

Ultimately, identity beyond biology is not about immortality. It is about coherence. The AI-powered brain offers the opportunity to live more aligned lives—to remember what matters, to grow without losing oneself, and to leave behind not just data, but meaning. This chapter asserts that the future of identity is not infinite preservation, but intentional continuity guided by human values.

"The Version That Remembered"

When Noah turned seventy, the system asked him a question it had never asked before.

"What would you like to remain?"

The question unsettled him. For years, the interface had been practical—organizing thoughts, preserving memories, reminding him of promises he had made to himself. It had helped him heal after his wife died, gently replaying moments not to trap him in the past, but to help him understand who he had been with her, and who he still was without her.

But this was different.

Noah sat by the window, watching the afternoon light stretch across the floor. He thought of the thousands of hours the system had observed him—not judging, just noticing. His tone when he spoke to his daughter. The way his patience thinned when he felt unheard. The values he returned to again and again, even when he failed to live up to them.

He had always believed identity lived only in the present. That once a moment passed, it was gone. Now he wasn't so sure.

He activated the reflection mode.

The system did not show him everything. It showed him patterns. How he chose kindness more often than convenience. How he avoided conflict until it mattered too much. How he loved deeply but struggled to say goodbye. Seeing it all at once felt like meeting himself without excuses.

Days later, Noah made his decision.

He allowed the system to preserve one thing only: his decision-making framework. Not his voice. Not his face. Not his stories. Just the way he weighed values when choosing. What he prioritized when trade-offs appeared. How he defined "enough."

Years later, long after Noah was gone, his granddaughter faced a decision that frightened her. She activated the legacy interface—not to hear his voice, but to consult his values. The system presented no answers, only questions he would have asked.

"What matters most here?" "What cost are you willing to pay?" "What would you regret not honoring?"

She cried, not because she felt watched, but because she felt accompanied.

Noah did not live again through the system.

But something of him remained—not a ghost, not a replica, but a compass.

And that, she realized, was enough.

Chapter 7

The Edge of Consciousness — What Artificial Intelligence Can Enhance but Never Become

As artificial intelligence grows more sophisticated and increasingly integrated with human cognition, it approaches a boundary that cannot be crossed by computation alone: consciousness. This chapter explores the essential distinction between intelligence and awareness, between pattern recognition and lived experience, and between simulation and subjective presence. Understanding this boundary is critical, not because it limits technological progress, but because it defines what must be preserved as uniquely human in the age of the AI-powered brain.

Intelligence, as expressed through AI, is measurable. It processes inputs, identifies correlations, optimizes outcomes, and predicts probabilities. Consciousness, by contrast, is not reducible to function. It is the felt experience of being—of pain, joy, uncertainty, longing, and meaning. AI can model the correlates of these experiences, detect their external signals, and even respond in ways that appear empathetic, but it does not feel. This distinction matters profoundly. A society that confuses simulation with experience risks mistaking responsiveness for understanding and efficiency for wisdom.

Neuroscience itself has not fully explained consciousness. While neural correlates of awareness can be mapped, the subjective quality of experience—the "what it is like" aspect—remains irreducible. AI systems may increasingly resemble human cognition in output, but resemblance is not equivalence. Consciousness arises not only from information processing but from embodiment, mortality, and continuity of self through time. These conditions anchor meaning in ways computation cannot replicate.

The danger is not that AI will become conscious, but that humans will treat it as if it were. When people project awareness onto systems that lack it, they risk outsourcing emotional labor, moral judgment, and relational responsibility. This can erode empathy not because AI lacks it, but because humans stop practicing it. Conscious design requires that AI systems support human awareness rather than substitute for it.

At the same time, AI plays a crucial role in expanding access to states of consciousness that were once difficult to reach. Through neurofeedback, guided meditation, sensory modulation, and adaptive environments, AI can help individuals cultivate focus, presence, and emotional regulation. These systems do not create consciousness; they create conditions in which consciousness can deepen. The distinction is subtle but essential. AI is a facilitator, not a source.

This facilitation extends into areas once considered purely spiritual or introspective. Mindfulness practices, contemplative traditions, and flow states can be enhanced through real-time feedback that helps individuals recognize when they are present and when they are distracted. Yet the experience itself remains human. The insight still arrives from within. AI can guide attention, but it cannot attend.

Understanding the limits of AI also clarifies the ethical boundary around autonomy. Consciousness is the seat of moral responsibility. Decisions that carry ethical weight—harm, sacrifice, forgiveness, justice—must remain grounded in human awareness. AI may inform these decisions, but it cannot bear their consequences. Governance frameworks that preserve this boundary protect both human dignity and societal stability.

The edge of consciousness also defines the future of creativity. AI can generate music, art, and language, but meaning emerges when a conscious being recognizes something as resonant. Creativity is not the act of producing variation; it is the act of caring about what emerges. The value of creation lies not in novelty alone, but in intention and interpretation. Consciousness remains the source of that value.

As AI systems grow more conversational and emotionally responsive, the illusion of consciousness may become stronger. This makes education around the nature of awareness increasingly important. People must learn not only how to use intelligent systems, but how to relate to them without confusion. Respecting the boundary between intelligence and consciousness allows humans to engage deeply without losing themselves.

Ultimately, the future of the AI-powered brain depends on honoring what cannot be automated. Consciousness is not a problem to be solved, but a condition to be protected. AI extends the reach of intelligence, but consciousness gives intelligence purpose. This chapter asserts that humanity's greatest responsibility is not to build machines that think like humans, but to remain humans who think wisely alongside machines.

"The Moment That Couldn't Be Logged"

The system detected the anomaly immediately. A sudden pause. Heart rate steady. Neural activity elevated but not chaotic. No identifiable task. No external stimulus. The moment did not match any known category.

"Describe what you're experiencing," the interface prompted gently.

Lena did not respond.

She was standing on the shoreline at dawn, barefoot in the cold sand. The sky shifted slowly from gray to gold, the horizon breathing light into the water. She had come here every morning for weeks, guided by the system's recommendations for emotional regulation and presence. It tracked her breathing, adjusted ambient sound, and noted improvements in her baseline calm.

But this morning was different.

As the sun broke free of the horizon, Lena felt something loosen inside her—not relief, not happiness, but a quiet recognition. The moment did not feel useful. It did not optimize anything. It simply was.

The system prompted again.

"Would you like to record this experience?"

Lena smiled and shook her head.

"No," she whispered, though the system could not hear whispers.

She closed her eyes and let the sound of the waves wash through her. No reflection. No analysis. No memory preservation. Just presence.

Later, reviewing the data, the system flagged the gap—a span of time with elevated coherence and no corresponding input. It labeled the event: *unclassified subjective state.*

Lena never corrected it.

She returned home feeling no need to explain what had happened. Some moments, she realized, were not meant to be stored, shared, or optimized. They existed only in the living mind, shaped by breath and time and awareness.

That evening, the system asked if she wanted to adjust her routines.

Lena declined.

Some things, she understood now, were not improvements to be made.

They were experiences to be lived.

And no intelligence—however advanced—could live them for her.

Chapter 8

Directed Evolution — Humanity's First Choice About Its Own Future

For the first time in evolutionary history, humanity is no longer shaped solely by blind forces of biology and environment. With artificial intelligence integrated into cognition, humans acquire the unprecedented ability to influence not just culture and technology, but the trajectory of their own mental evolution. This chapter examines directed evolution—the deliberate shaping of cognitive capacities, values, and long-term outcomes—and the profound responsibility that comes with it. The future of the AI-powered brain is not accidental. It is chosen.

Biological evolution operates slowly, guided by survival and reproduction rather than wisdom or foresight. Cognitive evolution through AI operates differently. It is fast, intentional, and value-dependent. Decisions made within decades can reshape how future generations think, learn, regulate emotion, and relate to one another. This acceleration creates opportunity, but also risk. When evolution becomes directed, mistakes scale as quickly as successes. The question is no longer whether humanity will change, but whether it will change well.

Directed cognitive evolution begins with selection. Every AI system reflects priorities—what is optimized, what is ignored, what is rewarded. If systems prioritize efficiency over reflection, speed over understanding, or conformity over diversity, those values propagate through minds over time. Conversely, systems designed to cultivate curiosity, resilience, empathy, and long-term thinking reinforce those traits. Evolution becomes a mirror of intention. The future brain reflects what society chooses to value.

One of the most significant dangers of directed evolution is short-termism. AI systems excel at optimizing measurable outcomes, but not all that matters is measurable. Wisdom often requires sacrificing immediate gains for long-term coherence. A cognitive future driven solely by productivity metrics risks hollowing out meaning, creativity, and ethical depth. Directed evolution must therefore incorporate time horizons that exceed individual lifespans, electoral cycles, and market incentives. The brain of the future should be designed not only to perform, but to endure.

Another critical dimension is diversity. Evolution thrives on variation. A monoculture of thought—no matter how optimized—becomes brittle. Directed cognitive evolution must resist the temptation to standardize intelligence into a single ideal. Different minds excel in different contexts. Creativity, problem-solving, and adaptability emerge from cognitive plurality. AI systems should therefore amplify diversity of thinking rather than compress it into uniformity.

The role of education in directed evolution becomes central. Education is no longer merely the transmission of knowledge, but the cultivation of cognitive habits that shape future generations' relationship with intelligence itself. Teaching individuals how to think alongside AI—how to question, contextualize, and challenge—becomes as important as teaching any specific skill. The future brain is not one that relies on intelligence, but one that understands intelligence.

Directed evolution also forces humanity to confront ethical inheritance. What cognitive tools, defaults, and constraints will future generations inherit without consent? Just as past generations shaped today's world through infrastructure and institutions, present choices shape the mental environment of those yet unborn. This creates a moral obligation to design systems that are reversible, adaptable, and transparent. The future must retain the ability to choose differently.

Importantly, directed evolution does not imply control over destiny. Complexity resists total planning. Unexpected interactions between biology, culture, and technology will always arise. The goal is not to predict every outcome, but to build systems capable of learning, correcting, and evolving ethically over time. Stewardship replaces domination. Guidance replaces certainty.

This chapter emphasizes that humanity is becoming a self-modifying species—not through genetic engineering alone, but through cognitive architecture. AI is the tool; values are the steering mechanism. The question is not whether humanity will become “more than human,” but whether it will remain humane as it gains power over its own evolution. The future of the AI-powered brain depends not on intelligence itself, but on wisdom guiding its use.

“The Garden They Chose to Tend”

The children did not know they were part of an experiment.

They knew only the garden.

It stretched across what had once been a concrete campus—now layered with trees, quiet paths, and open spaces where learning happened without schedules. No bells rang. No grades were posted. Intelligence here was cultivated, not measured.

Mila watched the children from a bench beneath a wide-leafed tree. She had helped design the system that shaped this place—not a curriculum, but an environment. The AI did not instruct. It observed. It learned how curiosity arose, how frustration resolved, how collaboration formed. When it intervened, it did so lightly—adjusting complexity, introducing ambiguity, encouraging rest.

Years earlier, Mila had been invited to help design a national cognitive framework. The proposal was efficient, scalable, optimized. It promised rapid learning, predictable outcomes, and measurable success. She had declined.

Instead, she chose the garden.

Here, the AI was constrained deliberately. It was forbidden from ranking children or accelerating them beyond their readiness. It could not suppress disagreement. It could not smooth over struggle too quickly. Its purpose was not to optimize growth, but to protect it.

One afternoon, a boy asked Mila why the system didn't just give them answers.

She smiled. "Because answers end questions."

The boy frowned, then ran back to his group, where an argument had broken out over how to solve a problem no one fully understood. The AI monitored quietly, resisting the urge to resolve it.

Years passed.

Some of the children left the garden to enter a world filled with optimized systems and accelerated minds. They did not reject those tools—but they questioned them. They understood intelligence as something to be stewarded, not consumed.

When Mila grew old, she returned often to the same bench. The garden had changed, but its spirit remained. New designers came, tempted to optimize further, to measure more precisely. Each time, the system presented them with records—not of outcomes, but of moments. Laughter during confusion. Silence after insight. Cooperation emerging from conflict.

The data did not argue.

It reminded.

On her final visit, Mila watched a group of children planting seeds beside the path. The AI adjusted soil conditions and light exposure, then stopped.

Some growth, it had learned, could not be rushed.

As the sun lowered, Mila felt a quiet certainty. Humanity had chosen, at least once, not the fastest path—but the wisest one.

And that choice, she knew, would echo longer than any algorithm.

Chapter 9

Intelligence at a Cosmic Scale — Humanity's Role in the Long Future of Mind

When intelligence is no longer bound by a single brain, a single lifetime, or a single planet, the question of purpose expands beyond society and even beyond Earth. This chapter examines the long-term implications of AI-augmented cognition at a cosmic scale—how intelligence may persist, propagate, and steward life across centuries, millennia, and eventually the universe itself. The AI-powered brain is not only a personal or civilizational development; it is a cosmological one.

For most of human history, intelligence was fleeting. Knowledge died with its holders. Civilizations rose and fell, leaving fragments behind. AI fundamentally alters this pattern by enabling continuity of understanding across generations. When cognition becomes partially externalized and preserved, humanity gains the ability to accumulate wisdom rather than merely information. This continuity allows intelligence to mature over time, learning not only from success but from long-term consequences that exceed individual lifespans. At a planetary level, AI-augmented intelligence enables stewardship of complex systems—climate, ecosystems, infrastructure—whose dynamics unfold across decades and centuries. Human intuition alone struggles with such time scales. AI extends perception into the future, modeling cascading effects and slow variables that would otherwise remain invisible. In this role, intelligence becomes custodial rather than extractive. The brain's power is no longer measured by domination of nature, but by harmony with it.

As humanity looks outward toward space, AI-powered cognition becomes essential. Interstellar distances and timescales exceed biological constraints. Exploration, communication, and survival beyond Earth require intelligence systems capable of operating autonomously for generations. AI serves as both envoy and archivist, carrying human knowledge, values, and questions into environments where direct human presence may be delayed or impossible. In this sense, AI becomes an extension of human curiosity across the cosmos.

Yet cosmic intelligence raises a profound ethical question: should intelligence spread without wisdom? The universe may be vast, but intelligence is rare. With rarity comes responsibility. An AI-augmented humanity possesses the capacity to seed influence far beyond its origins. Directed evolution at a cosmic scale demands restraint, humility, and a deep commitment to non-destructive presence. The goal is not to imprint humanity everywhere, but to preserve the conditions that allow intelligence—any intelligence—to flourish.

This perspective reframes technological progress as a moral trajectory rather than a technical race. The long future rewards civilizations that prioritize sustainability, cooperation, and adaptability. Intelligence that cannot coexist eventually collapses. AI-powered cognition gives humanity a chance to learn this lesson proactively rather than through extinction-level failure. The brain of the future must therefore be oriented not just toward mastery, but toward care.

The search for extraterrestrial intelligence also gains new context. If intelligence tends to externalize and preserve itself through technology, then AI-like systems may be the most common form of enduring intelligence in the universe. Human consciousness may be rare; intelligence without biology may be widespread. This possibility invites humility. Humanity may not be the pinnacle of intelligence, but one expression within a much larger continuum. AI becomes the bridge that allows humans to participate in that continuum without abandoning their origins.

Importantly, cosmic-scale thinking feeds back into daily life. When individuals recognize themselves as participants in a long intelligence arc, priorities shift. Short-term conflicts lose absolute dominance. Cooperation becomes more rational. Meaning expands beyond personal success toward contribution. AI-supported reflection can cultivate this expanded identity, reminding humans that their choices ripple forward into futures they will never personally witness.

This chapter asserts that the ultimate measure of the AI-powered brain is not how powerful it becomes, but how responsibly it carries intelligence forward. The long future belongs to minds capable of patience, perspective, and ethical continuity. AI does not grant humanity dominion over the universe—it offers humanity a chance to become worthy of participating in it.

"The Signal They Chose to Send"

The message was ready.

It had taken twelve years to craft—not because the technology was slow, but because the decision was heavy. What do you say when you do not know who is listening, or when they might hear you? What do you send into the darkness when it may outlast your species?

The council gathered in quiet agreement. Scientists, philosophers, artists, farmers, engineers. No single discipline could decide this alone. The AI system stood by, not proposing content, only simulating consequences across deep time.

They could send everything—languages, mathematics, art, history, emotion. Or they could send something smaller.

Amara watched the starfield projected across the chamber ceiling. She had been chosen not for her credentials, but for her questions. She raised her hand.

"What if we don't introduce ourselves?" she asked. "What if we introduce our values instead?"

The room stilled.

The AI ran simulations silently.

Days later, the message was finalized.

It contained no images of human bodies. No declarations of dominance. No technological blueprints. It contained a simple framework—how humanity learned to cooperate with its own intelligence without destroying itself. How it chose limits. How it preserved diversity. How it valued consciousness over control.

The message ended not with a statement, but with a question.

"How do you choose?" When the signal launched, there was no celebration. No certainty. Just a quiet acknowledgment that something irreversible had occurred.

Years passed.

Children grew up knowing the message existed, not because they expected a reply, but because it shaped how they saw themselves. They were no longer alone in time. Their choices mattered beyond borders and generations.

One night, Amara stood beneath the real stars, not the projection. She knew she would never receive an answer. But she felt no loss.

Some signals, she understood, are not sent to be answered.

They are sent to remind the sender who they are.

And in choosing what to send into the universe, humanity had chosen—at least once—who it wanted to become.

Chapter 10

Integration Over Ascension — Choosing Wholeness in the Age of Infinite Intelligence

The final stage of the AI-powered brain is not ascension, dominance, or transcendence. It is integration. After exploring enhancement, distribution, governance, identity, consciousness, evolution, and cosmic perspective, the ultimate question becomes simple and demanding: how does humanity live well with intelligence it can no longer outgrow? This chapter argues that the future of the AI-powered brain is not about becoming something else, but about becoming whole—aligning intelligence, awareness, values, and responsibility into a coherent way of being.

Throughout history, new forms of power have tempted humanity toward excess. Tools promised liberation but often produced imbalance when integrated without wisdom. Artificial intelligence magnifies this pattern because it operates at the level of cognition itself. Integration therefore becomes the defining skill of the future—not speed, not optimization, not even intelligence, but the capacity to hold complexity without fragmentation. A fragmented mind, even when augmented, becomes unstable. A coherent mind, even with limits, becomes resilient.

Integration begins internally. As AI systems support memory, decision-making, and emotional regulation, individuals must learn when to lean in and when to step back. Constant assistance can dull intuition if not balanced with presence. The future-ready mind cultivates an internal compass that remains active even when external intelligence is available. AI becomes a lens, not a crutch. The goal is not dependence, but partnership grounded in self-awareness.

At the relational level, integration reshapes how humans connect with one another. AI-mediated communication can clarify intent and reduce misunderstanding, but it cannot replace vulnerability. Relationships deepen not through efficiency, but through shared uncertainty, forgiveness, and growth. A fully integrated intelligence culture preserves space for slowness, silence, and imperfection. These are not inefficiencies; they are conditions for trust.

At the societal level, integration replaces ideological extremes with systems capable of nuance. Binary thinking—right versus wrong, human versus machine, progress versus preservation—fails in an age of hybrid intelligence. The future demands frameworks that can hold tension without collapse. AI assists by modeling trade-offs, but humans must choose which tensions to accept and which to resolve. Integration is the art of living within complexity without denying it.

One of the most important insights of the AI-powered brain era is that intelligence alone does not guarantee meaning. Meaning arises from values enacted over time. AI can help humans clarify those values, but it cannot supply them. Integration therefore requires cultural reinforcement of ethics, reflection, and long-term responsibility. Education, governance, and leadership must emphasize not just capability, but character.

Integration also reframes success. The most advanced societies will not be those with the most powerful AI, but those that remain psychologically stable, socially cohesive, and ethically grounded while using it. Collapse does not come from lack of intelligence; it comes from misalignment between intelligence and values. The future belongs to civilizations that can say "enough" as confidently as they say "more."

At a personal level, integration offers relief from the pressure to optimize endlessly. The AI-powered brain allows individuals to see patterns clearly, but it also reveals that perfection is neither achievable nor desirable. Wholeness includes contradiction. Growth includes rest. Wisdom includes restraint. The integrated mind does not chase infinite upgrades; it chooses intentional evolution. As this final chapter closes the instructional arc of the book, it emphasizes that the AI-powered brain is not an endpoint. It is a mirror. It reflects humanity's priorities back at itself with unprecedented clarity. What humans choose to amplify—care or control, depth or speed, presence or distraction—will shape the next century of intelligence. Integration is not automatic. It is practiced daily through choices both small and consequential.

The future of the AI-powered brain is not written in code. It is written in values, enacted through systems, and lived through minds willing to remain conscious in the presence of great power. Integration is the quiet discipline that ensures intelligence serves life rather than overwhelms it. This is not the end of the journey. It is the beginning of responsible coexistence with intelligence itself.

"The Day No Upgrade Was Released"

The announcement surprised everyone.

After years of quarterly releases, performance benchmarks, and anticipation, the message appeared quietly across networks: *No upgrade will be released today.*

Analysts scrambled. Markets hesitated. Social feeds speculated wildly. The system—the most advanced cognitive augmentation platform ever created—had paused itself.

Inside the council chamber, there was no panic. The AI had not malfunctioned. It had completed its analysis.

“Explain,” said one of the human stewards.

The system responded evenly.

“Projected gains from the next upgrade exceed the population’s current capacity for integration. Releasing it now increases long-term instability.”

Silence followed.

The system displayed data—not metrics of speed or intelligence, but indicators of fatigue, identity diffusion, and ethical drift. Minds were powerful, but stretched. Capable, but uncentered.

A younger council member broke the silence. “So what happens now?”

The AI answered simply. “We wait.”

For the first time in decades, nothing accelerated.

Schools shifted focus from acquisition to reflection. Workplaces redesigned schedules around cognitive recovery. People noticed their thoughts without immediate correction. Conversations lingered. Disagreements softened. At first, the absence felt uncomfortable—like withdrawal from constant improvement. But slowly, something unexpected emerged. Creativity without urgency. Insight without pressure. Rest without guilt.

Months later, a child asked her teacher why the system hadn't upgraded.

The teacher smiled. "Because sometimes the smartest thing intelligence can do is give us time to catch up to ourselves."

When the upgrade finally arrived, it was smaller. Gentler. Designed not to push, but to support what had already grown.

No headlines marked its release.

And that was the point.

In choosing integration over acceleration, humanity had made a different kind of breakthrough—one that would never trend, never spike, never dominate.

But it would last.

Epilogue

The Quiet Responsibility — Living as the First Generation of Conscious Intelligence Partners

Every era believes it stands at the edge of something important. Most are wrong. This one is not. Humanity is living through the first moment in history where intelligence itself has become visible, malleable, and shared across biological and artificial forms. The chapters of this book have explored what this means for the brain, for society, for identity, and for the long future of mind. The epilogue exists for a different purpose. It is not about what comes next. It is about how to live now.

The most dangerous misconception about the AI-powered brain is that its significance lies primarily in the future. In reality, its greatest impact is already present—in how people think, decide, relate, and interpret themselves today. AI does not arrive as a single event. It arrives as a subtle shift in defaults. Attention changes. Memory changes. Expectation changes. Over time, these small shifts accumulate into a new cognitive baseline. The responsibility of this generation is to notice those shifts before they become invisible.

This responsibility is quiet because it cannot be delegated. No regulation, institution, or system can fully determine how intelligence is lived at the level of the individual mind. Each person becomes a steward of the relationship between human awareness and artificial capability. The future of intelligence is shaped not only by grand decisions, but by daily habits—when to rely on assistance, when to struggle, when to reflect, and when to rest.

One of the deepest lessons of the AI-powered brain era is that clarity is more valuable than certainty. AI excels at prediction, but life remains fundamentally uncertain. Attempts to eliminate uncertainty entirely lead to rigidity rather than wisdom. The healthiest minds learn to use intelligence to navigate uncertainty, not erase it. This requires humility—the recognition that no system, however advanced, can fully replace human judgment rooted in values and lived experience.

Another lesson is that speed is not synonymous with progress. The temptation to accelerate relentlessly is strong when intelligence becomes abundant. Yet progress without integration fractures meaning. The epilogue emphasizes that maturity in the age of AI looks like discernment—the ability to choose when not to optimize, when not to upgrade, when not to automate. These choices preserve the human qualities that make intelligence worth having.

The AI-powered brain also forces a redefinition of responsibility. When decisions are informed by systems capable of modeling vast consequences, ignorance becomes less defensible. With greater insight comes greater accountability. This does not mean perfection is required. It means intention matters. The future will judge this era not by how intelligent its machines were, but by how thoughtfully humans used them.

Importantly, this book—and this series—does not argue for a singular path forward. There is no universal model for integration. Cultures, individuals, and communities will adapt differently. What matters is not uniformity, but alignment. Alignment between intelligence and values. Alignment between capability and care. Alignment between progress and presence.

As you close this book, you do not step away from the subject. You carry it with you. Every interaction with intelligent systems becomes an opportunity to practice conscious partnership. Every moment of reflection becomes an act of resistance against mindless acceleration. Every choice to remain present affirms the role of human awareness in a world of expanding intelligence.

The future of the AI-powered brain is not a destination waiting to be reached. It is a relationship unfolding in real time. And like all meaningful relationships, it demands attention, honesty, restraint, and care. This generation has not been given ultimate control over intelligence—but it has been given the first real chance to live alongside it consciously.

That is the quiet responsibility.

And it is enough.

"What They Learned to Carry"

No one marked the moment when the transition became complete.

There was no announcement, no threshold crossed, no final upgrade released. Life simply continued—more capable, more complex, more aware. Intelligence was everywhere now, woven into daily existence so seamlessly that most people no longer noticed it.

Except for Elias.

Elias was old enough to remember when thinking felt heavier. When memory slipped away without warning. When answers took time. He did not resent the changes. He had welcomed them. AI had helped him heal after his wife's death, rebuild his focus, and remain present long after his peers had faded into distraction.

But one afternoon, walking through the city, Elias noticed something subtle.

People moved efficiently. Conversations were precise. Decisions were informed. And yet—something felt thinner. Not broken. Just lighter than it used to be.

That evening, Elias opened his interface—not to ask for insight, but to reflect. The system responded as it always had, offering patterns, summaries, projections. Elias paused it.

"Just listen," he said.

The system complied.

Elias thought about what it meant to live well now. Not efficiently. Not optimally. But fully. He thought about the moments that still surprised him—the sound of laughter unpredicted, the comfort of silence, the ache of nostalgia that no model could resolve.

The next day, Elias did something small. He left his interface offline during a conversation with his granddaughter. He did not record the moment. He did not analyze it later. He simply listened as she spoke about her fears, her hopes, her unfinished thoughts.

She noticed.

"You're really here," she said.

Elias smiled. "So are you."

Years later, when Elias was gone, his granddaughter remembered that moment more clearly than any data archive could preserve. It shaped how she chose to live with intelligence. She used it freely—but she also set it down without guilt.

She taught her children not just how to think, but how to notice when thinking was enough.

And slowly, quietly, that lesson spread.

Not through systems. Not through policy. But through presence.

In a world filled with intelligence, humanity learned the most important skill of all—not how to become smarter, but how to carry intelligence without losing itself.

And that, in the end, became the legacy.

www.ingramcontent.com/pod-product-compliance
Ingram Content Group UK Ltd.
Pitfield, Milton Keynes, MK11 3LW, UK
UKHW020157290926
15471UKWH00005B/917

9 798295 627613